An OCD Life

By Fred Mletzko

chipmunkapublishing
the mental health publisher

By Fred Mletzko

Published by
Chipmunkapublishing
United Kingdom

http://www.chipmunkapublishing.com

Dedication

I would like to thank the following people for always being there throughout my life. My parents Al and Antoinette Mletzko, my great friends Jay Topper, Jean Wargo, Brandt Rousseaux, Larry Friedman, and Rebecca Friedman. My ex-wife Jean Boutot. My brother's Matt and Nick Mletzko, my Aunt Dianne Herbold, my Cousins Lisa Fallon and Shannon Ferrara, and my Cat buddies Julius and Shadow.

By Fred Mletzko

Chapter 1

It should have been the best day of my life. It was a beautiful afternoon. Sunny, a few clouds, temperatures in the 70's, and a slight breeze. I had worked obsessively for six years for this day. "The Captain" as I would be referred to from that day on. The day I take command of a Coast Guard Cutter, one of the toughest, most responsible and stressful jobs that exist. It's 1992.

We're tied up at the pier in Norfolk, VA. Unfortunately, my mind is obsessed with the fear of catching Aids. This was not a "normal" fear as I was not in a high risk group. I had taken this particular fear to extreme lengths due to what I would soon be diagnosed with OCD (Obsessive Compulsive Disorder). I got tested monthly and washed my hands constantly.

It was the first ship with a ½ male, ½ female crew, at least that's what I was told. I heard of a Navy patrol boat that beat us to it but I didn't research it. A duel crew would pose a number of new challenges for any Captain. The ship, USCGC Pea Island, was named after the only all-African American Coast Guard Station, Pea Island, on the outer banks of North Carolina. It was black history month which is why we are holding this ceremony in February. I am one of the youngest officers to ever hold this position. The Coast Guard no longer puts people in charge of a 110 ft Coast Guard Cutter at such a young age. I'm 24. Half the crew is older than I am. I'm the only officer.

I studied obsessively while at the Academy. I remember one time sitting on the toilet taking care of business, and studying a Chemistry book on my lap. I used every second of every day to study. The only break I gave myself was going out and getting wasted on Saturday nights. But, no matter how late I stayed up, or how much I drank, I always woke up at 7:00 AM the next morning and continued my studies. I graduated 3rd in my class with a 3.79 GPA. I was confident and succeeding.

During my tour in Hawaii, I was constantly working. Six, seven days a week. Even in 25 ft. seas. In rough seas, most of the crew spent their time in bunks. I spent mine either on the computer or on the Bridge of the ship. Nothing could keep me from my main goal.

I had worked hard on my speech. The words came out of my mouth, smooth. I wasn't thinking about that though. I was obsessing over the fact that I shook hands with a number of people that day. What if there was a cut on their hand and a cut on my hand and the cuts touched each other and the person had Aids, would I catch it, etc. on and on the fear constantly in my thoughts. Did I see any cuts? I don't have any on my hand but maybe the blood could seep through the skin. Oh no, what if that was true! Does the audience notice that I keep looking at my right hand?

I've seen and done many things in my life. I received my diploma at the U.S. Coast Guard Academy from President George H. W. Bush. The academy was the hardest school to get into in the whole country according to U.S. News and World Report. I Led the league in scoring in basketball my high school senior year and was named MVP of the league. My first Coast Guard tour of duty was Hawaii because of how high I graduated in my class at the Academy. I've seen space shuttle launches at night, was in Times Square NYC during 9/11, and was named Teacher of the Year and Coach of the Year at a military high school. I received three promotions over three years as a manager of IT (information technology). I was given nine awards and five nominations as an amateur movie film producer. I saved over 1,000 lives as a Coast Guard Officer. I'm the center of a book called "Pararescue" about one of the

Search and Rescue cases. The list goes on and on.

However, while achieving these goals, I was constantly tormented by OCD. According to the IOCDF, "OCD is a seriously life-limiting, soul-sucking mental illness that infects every word, every decision and every relationship and steals your personal peace. Inside one's mind, a battle rages against unwanted thoughts and fears that flourish uncontrollably and dominate one's existence."
Let's just say it's pure hell and leave it at that.

Pictured with President George H. W. Bush during my graduation from the U.S. Coast Guard Academy.

Graduation day. From Left to Right, My cousin Shannon Howell, my cousin Lisa Howell, me, my Aunti Dianne Howell, and my Mom Antoinette Mletzko.

Chapter 2

I'm living on Governor's Island, New York (1/2 mile South of Manhattan), and I work at the Atlanta Area Command Center. It's 1994. We are in charge of ½ of the entire Atlantic Ocean. I'm working a Search and Rescue case that will be the subject of a book called "Pararescue" by Michael Hirsch. 31 people are onboard and getting ready to abandon ship in 50 ft. seas. I work this case intensely for 24 hrs straight.

The ship was called the Salvadore Allende. A 450-foot bulk cargo ship out of the Ukraine. The ship had been in rough seas for two days with the wind reaching 60 mph. It became unstable when the cargo shifted after encountering a rogue wave around 100 ft high.

We divert numerous ships. This is not the easiest thing to do as they are on a tight schedule and when they divert to help with a Search and Rescue case it can cost the owners millions of dollars. Fortunately, most of them do divert to help save lives. It's the code of the sea.

Throughout the night, we receive continuous updates from the ships enroute the Salvadore

Allende. The closest one will arrive around 6:30AM. The crew is waiting until the last minute to abandon ship. At around 6:10AM, we receive word that the ship is sinking and everyone is jumping overboard. There is still 20 minutes left until help arrives.

The crew had to actually go into the water because the rafts hadn't inflated yet. There is usually a pressure switch so when the ship sinks to a certain depth, the rafts inflate and rise to the surface.

A survivor later reveals that he watched his shipmates sink into the ocean one after the other. They were too tired and sea sick to make it to the rafts. When you are in heavy seas, you experience a type of fatigue that is hard to explain. It's awful. I experienced it regularly during my four plus years at sea.

Why couldn't the ship last another half hr? What a disaster. A sinking feeling hits the pit of my stomach. I walk back to my apartment wondering why this happened. My heart goes out to their family and friends.

Although a success to even save two lives, it feels like a huge failure to me. Only 20 more minutes needed out of hours of waiting.

At the same time in my life, I'm obsessed with the fear of being arrested for something I didn't do. I wouldn't touch anything in the grocery store because I was afraid that if the item ended up at a crime scene, and my fingerprints were on it, I could somehow be blamed for it. I liked it when I could wear gloves in the winter (although I hate the cold) because I could actually pick up items without worrying about putting my fingerprints on anything. I felt so free.

The view from my apartment is of the prison on Governors Island that is no longer used. How ironic! It's run down, scary looking, and a constant reminder of my fears.

I saw a CSI episode where a cat hair showed up at a crime scene and it was traced back to the owner. I owned two cats. What if one of their hairs showed up at a scene and as a result I was blamed for the crime? I vacuumed my apartment incessantly to ensure all cat hairs were collected. I even taped off my cats on a regular basis. Actually used roller tape and ran it across my cats daily. My cats put up with it because they were intensely devoted to me. Julius and Shadow were the best companions I could ever ask for (Julius was named after the cat in the movie "Twins" starring Arnold Schwarzenegger). Of course, I worried about them constantly. I had returned from work frequently because I thought I left the balcony door open. This thought would just stick in my head and feel like someone was scratching my brain with a nail. An hr. wasted each time. Of course, the door was always locked. But I just couldn't be confident of it. The OCD wouldn't let me, ever.

Chapter 3

I board the Hudson Line train out of Beacon just like every morning. It's 2001. Each day, the commute takes me 2 hrs. and 15 minutes one way. It's the same process every day. Try to find a seat. Wait for the conductor to come by and show him your ticket. Either listen to headphones or read a book. Look at the Hudson River on the way down. Head past Harlem and see the progress being made there. Enter the dark tunnel and arrive at Grand Central Station. Wait in line to leave the train. Start walking towards and past the NBC morning show on my way to work.

I'm heading to my job as an IT Manager at Proskauer Rose LLC, a law firm with clients like Madonna and Patrick Ewing. It's a job I hate with every cell in my body.

I'm listening to Howard Stern on my headphones as I walk into Times Square. Robin pipes in that a plane hit the Twin Towers. Ok, must be some kind of freak accident. Then she announces that a second plane has hit. Uh oh, not sure what's going on, but this doesn't sound good. My heart sinks.

I went into the law firm and started watching tv with everyone else. All of a sudden, one of the towers collapses. Everyone is in shock. Then the second one goes down. No one speaks anymore. People don't know what to say. It doesn't feel real.

Grand Central Station is shutdown. My boss and I decide to walk from 46th street to 125th street in Harlem to catch the train out of the city. The streets are eerily quiet. No police or firefighter sirens…they are already at the site of the tragedy. No one bothers each other as we are too shocked to do anything but walk. We watch the smoke from the city during the train ride north.

My anxiety level is higher for the next few months. I go back into therapy to discuss it. The tics are really bothering me. Shaking my head constantly for no apparent reason. I'm taking medication. I have a good Dr. but he decides to take a job in a hospital emergency room. I need to find a new doctor again. Unless you have tried to find a Dr., you don't know how hard it is to find a good one. Here goes the search again.

My family and friends contact me to find out if I'm ok. They know I work in the city. I'm not sure what to say to them other than thank God I was not in or near the twin towers. But I'm far from ok. What a disaster. I can't believe this has happened. The world will never be the same.

Chapter 4

We're listening to the countdown of the Space Shuttle. It's 1993. 60 seconds until launch. We're covering up to three miles offshore off the launch site at night. The crew is on edge due both to the excitement of seeing the nighttime launch, and the job of keeping any boats or vessels out of the zone. If one gets in, the launch is delayed and we take the blame. We would end up on the 6:00PM news.

A nighttime launch is one of the coolest events you could ever see. It's so bright you have to shield your eyes. It's like the Sun is blasting off from the launch pad straight up. Everything shakes, including the ocean. Such raw power at work.

30 minutes before launch, I sight a small boat traveling along the shore and about to enter the zone. I radio it in to Control and they acknowledge. Probably didn't care about it or worry too much. Just keep an eye on it they tell me. We watch it motor along the shore and leave the zone.

This is our 5th launch so other than it being nighttime, we have done this before. I hear 30 seconds to launch and realize that we are still in the zone. We need to get out. At the same time, the Engineer calls the bridge and tells me we need to shut down one of the engines because of an oil leak. I disregard what he recommends and push both throttles down to ensure we get out of the zone. We just make it out. The head engineer asks me why I didn't do as he recommended. I explain in detail what happened. We both agree that the action taken was the appropriate one. We have a solid working relationship. He doesn't know that I have severe OCD. I don't even know that yet. All I know is I can't control my mind and I'm insane.

I will soon become severely depressed. The type of depression where you feel like there is no hope. I live with two Dr's in a house on the beach. This was not the best choice because I had a great view of the ocean…a view of basically where I work every day so I didn't receive a break. Imagine that…living on a beach actually causing a person stress.

In any event, upon my return from the space shuttle launch, one of the Dr's gives me Paxil. It's a new anti-depressant that's about to hit the market. I take it and a week later I feel incredible. No anxiety. Does this stuff really work that well? I would continue to take it for the rest of my life, at least up until this writing. It saves me from blowing my brains out in my cabin with a 9mm pistol, so I guess it works.

Chapter 5

The U.S. Coast Guard Academy is one of the hardest schools in the country to get into. It's 1989. During the first year, I was obsessed with the ridiculous fear of failing out of school, among many other things. One of my compulsions was repeating a phrase in my mind whenever I felt any anxiety towards it. This was not something I could control. Unfortunately, my anxiety was high and I was at the point where I couldn't stop repeating it, something similar to "The Aviator", the time at the end when Howard Hughes (DiCaprio) repeats over and over again, "It's the way of the future…the way of the future…the way of the future", as he throws his hat down in disgust because he can't stop saying it.

So this one basketball game, I'm repeating a similar phrase over and over again while trying to listen to the coach. The one from "The Aviator" is the least terrifying to me, so I'll use that one to explain.

Coach: "Fred, you play point guard today and guard #12."

Fred: "Ok Coach", My head "It's the way of the future, the way of the future, way of the future……."

Coach: "Full court press from the beginning, let's go"

I get the ball inbounds, "it's the way of the future, the way of the future…" and hit a layup while I'm fouled hard to the floor "it's the way of the future, the way of the future…".
Standing at the free throw line to finish off the three point play "Way of the future, of the future" ….."SHUTUP"……and I hit the shot.
Coach at Halftime – "Fred, pay attention, you have three fouls in the first half, and two of them were stupid…"
"Way of the future…way of the future, of the future………"
"I don't understand you. Some games you're on. Others, you just don't seem to be focusing…"
"The way of the future, way of the future".
"What did I just say?"
"Coach, you were saying I need to be more consistent and focus better…"
"Way of the future, of the future, of the future………………"
"Good, I'm glad you're listening!!!"
"Way of the future….." ……."STOP PLEASE".

We win the game. "Good job guys. Fred, I saw better focus in the second half"
"It's the way of the future…" Thanks Coach
"Way of the future, of the future…"
After the game, I get ready for the evening meal "Way of the future…." and afterwards

head to the library to study for three hours. During all three hours "The way of the future, of the future" continues in my head until lights out "way of the future, of the future…" I'm tired from the game and from studying, but my mind won't shut up. I try to fall asleep during the next two hours, praying for this to stop "The way of the future…", until my brain has somehow burnt out for the day and I fall asleep. I dream about my fear of not making it to formation on time, while my mind continues, "The way of the future…" in my dream! I wake up too tired to even think. For 45 minutes, my mind is quiet. "Maybe today's the day my mind stops with this phrase! I'm sure my grades will be fine".

10 minutes later, I'm in the bathroom stall with my head in my hands as my mind starts all over again "The way of the future, way of the future, way of the future…." I chastise myself for shedding tears, hold it in as best I can, and start my day over again by heading to class "The way of the future……………………………………………… ………………."

6 days later, it stops. I get a 3 day break from my mind, until my next OCD episode. Who knows what it will be this time. Pinching contact lenses, shaking my head, constantly asking my professors for assurance, walking

through certain hallways only on the right and counting the steps, etc. I don't know, but I put on a happy face and continue with my life. Three hours later. "It's the way of the future, way of the future, way of the future…please no, please stop, oh God what is wrong with me…".

Basketball Court at U.S. Coast Guard Academy.

Chapter 6

We all need to pass through metal detectors. It's 1989, graduation day at the Coast Guard Academy. President Bush has picked our Academy as the one to visit this year on graduation day. President Reagan came last year. Two years in a row we had the President. I don't think a President visited the same Academy two years in a row accept maybe West Point. We beat out Air Force Academy and the Naval Academy. They were not happy. Graduation causes you to reflect on your time spent there. The Academy is very challenging. Only 6% of the applicants gained admission in my year 1985. There is a 60% attrition rate. The first year is the toughest. For example, eating breakfast, lunch, and dinner was very difficult. As a freshman, you had to sit on the first 3 inches of the chair with your back straight. You keep your eyes "in the boat", fixed straight ahead at the freshman across from you. If you look down at your plate or anywhere other than straight ahead the punishment could be up to 100's of pushups. You had to bring the eating implement straight up and then move it at a 90 degree angle towards your mouth. After a while, you can almost see your plate without looking at it. But in general, you eat very little and lose a lot of weight 4th Class Year (Freshman Year).

In the barracks, you walk in the middle of the hallway, arms down vertical tight against your thighs, and you look straight ahead. Freshmen spend a great deal of time "braced up" against the wall. You stand with your back to the wall, heels touching it, and you bend your neck so that it touches the wall as well. Most Swabs (4th Class) couldn't do this at first, but eventually, our necks would bend. Just try to imagine that. Your spine actually bends and takes on a new shape. I don't know whether they still do that today, but in my time, I was absolutely straight from the shoulders to the back of the head.

As soon as the seniors graduate, you are promoted to 3rd Class. Sophomore year. No one bothers you, and you don't have any responsibilities yet except your academics. Juniors are in charge of the Freshmen, and Seniors are in charge of the entire Corps of Cadets.

After summer training, returning to the Academy with shoulder boards sporting a nice diagonal gold line separating you from the new Swabs is one of the best feelings I have ever experienced. No more sitting on the edge of the chair during breakfast, lunch, or dinner. You could actually sit there relaxed and have a conversation with your classmates. No more bracing up in the barracks. No more being at the bottom rung. Oh my God, what a fantastic time that was.

Chapter 7

My first tour of duty is in Hawaii. It's 1989. Two of the best years of my life. I had strong goals, was young and tan, and went to the gym regularly. We traveled to all of the Hawaiian Islands, and others' in the Pacific including Midway Island, Palmyra Island, and American Samoa.

I worked my ass off on the ship, and partied hard with my friends. The night life in Waikiki was wonderful, and there were a large number of nurses looking for military men. It was heaven on earth.

Hawaii is perfect. Not the people, they are far from perfect, but Hawaii itself. Here's an example. You are laying out on one of their beautiful beaches. You start getting a little hot, and wish things would cool off for a few minutes. As soon as you wish this, a small cloud blocks the sun. After a couple of minutes, you decide you've had enough shade and you want your sun back. The cloud then moves away from the sun. It's as if the Islands have a mind of their own and are ready to serve your every need and desire.

25 years later, my stay in Hawaii turns into a nightmare. There is a rather large drug distribution network in Hawaii, especially in Waikiki on the island of Oahu. They cater

mostly to the tourists I'd imagine. A rumor starts that I am an undercover cop. I keep running into the same person over and over again, and eventually that person is put in prison (or back in prison). I was blamed for this. I was the subject of constant mean looks and cat calls. I was watched constantly by this network. They would take pictures of me and text them throughout their group. It's surprising how large a group of people is, and how you don't notice it unless they think you're an undercover cop. Was this my OCD/Paranoia acting up? Partly yes. But this harassment forced me to leave Hawaii. My favorite place in the world was gone because of my OCD, and because of these drug dealers. It was just as well. It was not the same as 1989.

I decided to move to Las Vegas. Unfortunately, this network seemed to have connections there, and everyone seemed to know who I was (drug dealers I mean). This is what caused me to get very drunk one night and take a whole bottle of Seroquel. I ended up in intensive care for 3 weeks. I didn't die, and I can only assume it is because I'm meant to still be here.

One of the biggest surprises of this stay was that they still had my wallet. Go figure.

Chapter 8

I'm in the dugout of my girls Varsity Softball Team and I have déjà vu. It's 2008. We are in the Championship game and it's the last inning. Three outs and we win. It will be the first time a girls' varsity team wins a league title in the history of the school. I'm 'ticking', shaking my head constantly due to the anxiety I feel. I have a quick meeting with the team and the girls take the field.

I'm on a ton of medications. 120 mg of Paxil. 400 mg of Luvox. Xanax 0.5 mg as needed, and I need it a few times per day. 300 mg of Lamictal. 150 mg of Lamotrigine. 50 mg of Armour Thyroid. I feel zoned out most of the time. But not today.

It's a beautiful day. Sunny with a few clouds, temperature in the 70's. The perfect day for a softball game. A perfect day for our softball game.

The girls get the first out right away. On a hit, the shortstop gets hit in the ankle and needs to come out of the game. Now the second out, a popup to the outfield, and finally the third out which I didn't even see. The place goes nuts. We can't believe it. Everyone is hugging each other and crying.

The Superintendent of the school will later describe the day as clouds opening up and the hand of God reaching down and blessing us. I definitely believe that. It didn't feel real. It still doesn't feel real to this day; 10 years later. It was an incredible day…and I was fortunate to have experienced it. Every coach dreams of winning a title, no matter how often they say it's not about that.

The Massanutten Military Academy Girls' Softball Championship Team.

At the Sports banquet I'm named Coach of the Year. In just a few weeks, I'll be named Teacher of the Year by student vote, a wopping

50%. I work my ass off all the time, but I'm shocked that this happens. I'm not sure I'm hard enough on the kids both in the classroom and on the sports field. Maybe I'm more of a much needed break from the rigors of a Military High School. I'm not sure.

I drive home that night and imagine taking my seatbelt off and driving into the abutment of a bridge. I have these thoughts all the time. It's called suicidal ideation. I never had these thoughts before being on Meds. The meds put these thoughts in your head and I believe this is why the suicide rate is so high, especially among Veterans…a wopping 22 per day. It's so sad. I wish I could help. Maybe writing this book will help, although I'm not sure how.

Chapter 9

I'm living in Hawaii again and I start taking acting lessons. It's 2014. Before the lessons start, there is a movie shoot going on at a local store. I am very excited to be on set. It's an exciting feeling. I'm picked to be an extra in the shoot.

I can't receive any income due to my status with Veteran Affairs. As a result, it's very difficult to do anything in show business because they are required to pay you no matter what you do. You could act, be an extra, work the camera, etc. and because of the unions they must pay you.

I showed up one morning at an audition for a Reality TV Show. They were paying everyone $40 and I told them that I couldn't take it. I was concerned about their record keeping so I left. I have to consider my participation in acting a hobby.

Of course, you can always donate money for a Producer title in the movie. I'm a Co-Executive Producer for a short film called "Reservations for Three" which turns out to be an award bonanza. If you search my name on IMDb, you will find that I have participated in many films, some by volunteering to do some work, others by donations. I flirt with the idea of moving to Hollywood and trying to make it as an actor.

Unfortunately, I'm not very good. The OCD is part of the reason, although I can't blame it all on that.

Chapter 10

I'm teaching Chinese students Advanced Calculus and Advanced Statistics. It's 2012. I am also the Department Head of the Math Department, and the basketball coach. My students are incredibly bright, and it's an honor to be their teacher. This is quite the promotion as I've never been a department head before. I have five teachers who report to me.

I lose 60 lbs and look gaunt due to the stress of the job. Most of the students are smarter than I am, and they know it. I'm obsessed with the idea that I'm not good enough, like an itch in my brain that I can't scratch, and I bother the Assistant Dean on a regular basis to reassure me that I'm good enough to teach them.

I'm hospitalized early in the school year. I spend a week in a psychiatric unit. I didn't want to die, but felt like I was stuck between a rock and a hard place. I'm unable to quit this job because I'm not someone who gives up easily. In April, I really start to deteriorate. I'm having suicidal thoughts. I'm asked to resign and I do. The students take the AP exams at the end of the school year. Their performance is consistent with how the past students did on the exam. I taught them well. All of my worrying and stress were for nothing. That's probably a good description of what OCD is.

Chapter 11

I shoot the ball and score. It's 1985. My senior year in High School. I lead the basketball league in scoring. In fact, I can pretty much score at will as I've played basketball my whole life and I've become fairly good. It's the third game that I've scored 30+ pts and I have the team's last 12 pts in 3 minutes to win the game. I lead the team in rebounds and assists. I end up winning the league's MVP Award.

I can't stop squeezing my contact lenses. I squeeze them all the time until they feel right, which is never. I'm doing this constantly. I do this during basketball games and wonder what people are thinking. I don't know why I pinch my contact lenses. It reminds me of when I was younger and my braces would be tightened. My teeth would hurt and I would press them together so it hurt more and I was in tears.

A part of me exists that absolutely seems to hate the other part. It's a constant conflict and it causes me endless anxiety. I'm tormented constantly. This may be the Core of OCD, but I'm not sure. My baby sister died of SIDS when I was 14 months old, so maybe I blame myself subconsciously. It's been discussed thoroughly in therapy but I'm not sure I'm any better for it.

I'm nervous every time I go to school. Seeing those yellow lights on the Bus coming up the street to my house immediately sends my anxiety through the roof. I pretend I'm cool and aloof at school, but a thunderstorm of activity is happening in my stomach. The anxiety, along with my perfectionistic nature, create OCD, at least this is my theory.

Chapter 12

As of this writing, I spent a week in the psychiatric ward only three months ago, and 8 weeks in an intensive outpatient treatment program immediately following that. There are good days and bad. The good days are ok, and the bad days are really bad. But, with new advances in modern science every day, I'm hopeful for a better future. I've experienced a lot of interesting events throughout my life, but with OCD constantly at my side. It's like a companion that doesn't like you very much, and never shuts up, 24 hrs a day. Hopefully, modern science will come up with a solution. I beg of you, over and over and over...again.

www.ingramcontent.com/pod-product-compliance
Lightning Source LLC
Chambersburg PA
CBHW022349040426
42449CB00006B/787